Praise for Y

"From college to present day, I observed this mountain climber, energizer bunny, prolific mentor, and happiest person on earth achieve endeavor after endeavor. We are so fortunate to have her describe the head space that has moved her to successful entrepreneur, civic advocate, business incubator, philanthropist. *Take notes!*"

—MARILYN D. WILLIAMS, ESQUIRE, DIRECTOR, CONSULTING

"*Yes, You* Are *Able* takes us on an inviting and encouraging motivational journey. We are inspired to recognize our potential and even more importantly, intentionally and expectantly tap into our potential so that we can build the foundation and the pathway for our goals, all on solid ground. I felt positive and hopeful and like I had a real-life partner in reading it."

—VELEKA PEEPLES-DYER, ESQUIRE

"Theresa is a phenomenal woman and has undertaken a full court press with all of her goals and dreams. In the thoughtful and passionate writing of *Yes, You* Are *Able*, she is the experienced coach you need to climb any mountain in your life and reach your full potential."

—DIANE RICHARDSON, HEAD COACH TOWSON STATE UNIVERSITY WOMEN'S BASKETBALL

"If you need a push, this is it! Theresa captures the perfect balance of encouragement and personal storytelling to make this a total win in motivation for both your personal and professional worlds."

—DR. TAMARA NALL, CEO, THE LEADING NICHE, *USA TODAY* & *WALL STREET JOURNAL* BESTSELLER

"*Yes, You* Are *Able*" is a must-read. It is powerfully *inspiring*! Theresa's candid and personal examples of challenges and peaks, as well as those of others, are so relevant. She provides thoughtful tools to move you forward in your climb, all while feeling that she is right beside you. From beginning to end, you are made to feel 'You *Are* Able' and the climb is doable, regardless of the obstacles. Her inspirations move you from ABC (always believing you can) to knowing ATP (all things are possible). I am so blessed to have her as my companion on the climb!"

—DR. OLIVIA WHITE, VICE PRESIDENT FOR STUDENT LIFE
AND DEAN OF STUDENTS, HOOD COLLEGE, RETIRED

"Theresa shares lessons and wisdom that she has learned throughout her life that will encourage the reader to ask themselves the right questions yet at the same time persuading them to 'keep on keeping on.' Her positive and practical approach can be applied to so many life and career situations that most entrepreneurs experience."

—KARLYS KLINE, WOMEN'S GIVING CIRCLE, FOUNDER

"The book we all need in 2021. *Yes, You* Are *Able* gives a comprehensive step-by-step path forward into our wildest dreams and goals."

—TYRICA HENDRICKS DUCKETTS, ENTREPRENEUR,
PHILANTHROPIST, WORLD TRAVELER

"I'm so glad Theresa wrote *Yes, You* Are *Able*, because I've finally found someone who is talking to me and walking with me as I go after my dreams and goals."

—TAIYA TRIBIT-HACKEY, DIRECTOR, SALES
AND CUSTOMER EXPERIENCE

Yes, You Are Able

THERESA HARRISON

Edited by Rebecca Mitchell

Your day is coming.

*This book is dedicated to my parents,
Ben and Evelyn Williams.*

*They climbed mountains their entire life
and taught all us children how to prepare
for the climb.*

I love you and thank you!

Contents

Acknowledgments

I really just want to start by thanking Rebecca Mitchell for helping me fulfill my dream of writing this book. She willingly shared her gift of time and bought into my dream and vision from day one.

Though I'm sure she might have wanted to strangle me at times, she put up with me with unbelievable patience, steady encouragement, and unwavering support. Instead of leaving me stranded on this steep mountain, she laced up tighter and continued moving forward. She was prepared for this climb.

She held me accountable to get this work done, offered inspiration and guidance, and dove into the nuances of the text and stories to ensure they conveyed my message. She pushed me to clarify thoughts and concepts, to explore particular facets of my analogies, and to explain the rationale of every chapter.

Rebecca made this journey and destination worthwhile. I look forward to all the other mountains I will climb with her. I appreciate her more than I can actually express in words and am amazed I get to work with someone so committed, giving, truthful, and willing to be a part of my story.

Thank you Rebecca!

Foreword

Captain Gail Harris

UNITED STATES NAVY, RETIRED

In the late 90s, I found myself coming to the end of my turbulent, but—through God's grace—ultimately successful naval career. I had been the first woman and/or African American in most of my jobs. I had also reached the rank of Captain. Jumping ahead a little, when I retired at the end of 2001, I was the highest ranking African American female in the Navy. Despite that, I was wondering what my next step would be. Would the success strategies that had served me well in the military also work in the civilian world?

Since I wore a uniform every day to work, I was also clueless about some basic things, like what types of clothing to wear in work and social environments and, honestly, how to even conduct myself appropriately in social settings. For many of my jobs, I was one of the few women in the organization, so my social skills left much to be desired. In my efforts to prove I could handle being in a mostly male environment, I frequently used my sense of humor to both defuse situations and to fit into the military culture of the time. Practical jokes and teasing were common tools many used to break the tension in a job where a crisis or war could break out on any given day. I didn't know much, but even I knew that once I left the military, the civilian workplace would have a different dynamic.

My father always told me there were two things you could do about a problem: something or nothing. I decided to do something. I went on a cruise focused on providing African Americans a venue to meet and network with other successful professionals. It was one of the smartest things I ever did. On the cruise, I encountered many well-known politicians, entrepreneurs, entertainers, athletes, etc., but one of the people who stood out the most was Theresa Harrison. She was accomplished, kind, gracious, and welcoming, and over the years kindly and tactfully helped me knock off my rough edges. She was a tremendous role model and was successfully navigating what is now called work-life balance. When we met, she had already built a successful multi-million-dollar company from the ground up and would go on to develop other successful businesses. She was happily married and raising two daughters, who would go on to blaze successful paths of their own, in school and industry. She and her husband's parenting skills were awesome to watch over the years, and I always teased her that she needed to write a "How to Parent" book.

Growing up, we're not taught that with success comes many challenges. We will encounter many obstacles and setbacks throughout our career. As I watched Theresa over the years, I think the phrase that best describes her is the famous Ernest Hemingway quote: "Courage is grace under pressure." She successfully overcame many challenges, from being one of the early woman-owned businesses to work in the defense and intelligence industries to overcoming rivals' roadblocks to managing an aggressive form of cancer. When cancer knocked on her door she told it, "*Get out! You are not welcome here.*" I have never seen someone fight that awful disease with such grace, determination, and pure grit.

As I entered my new life, Theresa was always there for me. This took many forms—from letting me know that based on my experience, I was viewed as a key hire and my salary should reflect this, to surprising me and showing up at my first speaking engagement and making sure my wardrobe fit the occasion. She gave me invaluable feedback on how to tailor my talks to a non-military audience. These recommendations may seem like small things to many, but they were invaluable to me. Theresa is the kind of leader, who not only opens the door to go where few women have gone before, but also holds it open for others to follow. She has imparted many valuable lessons to me over the years and I am thrilled that she is now going to share her wisdom and hard-earned lessons with the rest of the world.

I encourage you to sit down, relax, and remember to fasten your seatbelts as she guides you through the mountains you will climb as you reach your goals. Fear not the inevitable valleys, she'll show you how to climb back up the next mountain!

Introduction

Packing Our Bags

"I got my start by giving myself a start."

MADAME CJ WALKER

Hey, Friend!

Good morning, afternoon, evening, or good night! If we haven't had the chance to meet in person, I am Theresa. I am a wife, a mom, a daughter, a friend, and a business owner. I am just an ordinary person, who—through the right mindset—has lived an extraordinary life, and I want you to do the same!

Life is full of opportunities, if we just embrace the journey. I want to invite you to travel with me, climb the mountains of your life, and realize the dreams you have always wanted to achieve. Consider me your adventure partner! We'll pack our bags, train for the climb, help you reach your dreams, and have a lot of fun along the way.

I wish you were here with me so we could sit on the couch in my family room, lay out our supplies, and dream together. By the way, I always have good food and something to drink to prepare for our journey!

In this adventure, we'll explore the highest peaks you've always wanted to reach. I want to hear about all that you envision your life to be. What dreams have you left lingering for years? What goals have you thought you may never complete? What challenges have come to define you instead of refine you? It's time that we talk it out, reset our vision, and push through to all that we are created to be and are able to do. And I'll tell you this: What you're able to do—it's far more than you can even imagine at this point!

Your day is *coming*! It is *never* too late to start, it's never too late to pick up again and continue, it's never too late to reassess, it's never too much to finish, and never too

> *Your day is coming! It is never too late to start.*

big of a dream to accomplish. Your time is *now*, and it begins with a shift in your mindset.

Yes, there might be challenges. Yes, there may be times when you're tired or worn out. Yes, you might face unexpected obstacles. But that's what I'm here for! Throughout this book, I want you to feel like we are on the mountains of life together. I am climbing with you, and even more so, I am *preparing* for the climb with you. We are in this together, from start to finish. I want to share some tools to help you with your journey, and tips I have learned over the years to keep you pushing through to reach your highest summits.

During our time together, you'll learn a bit about me, hear my stories, and then I want to hear all about you and your stories! When it's all said and done and we're sitting on the mountaintop

Introduction

enjoying the view. I hope it's just the beginning for you. I hope that the skills and lessons you learn here can change your mindset and change your life. I hope the highest peaks just keep growing, the views keep becoming more and more beautiful, and years down the road I can hear all about the adventures you were able to have.

It's not too late to get started. This is only the beginning, and I am so excited to be on this adventure with you. I got your back!

Packing Your Bags

To prepare for this journey, let's pack our bags! As you go through this adventure, the best things to have are:

1. A journal to record your thoughts and answer questions along the way

2. Your favorite snacks to keep you going

3. An open mindset to dream the seemingly impossible

Chapter 1

Building Your Mountains

"If you set goals and go after them with all the determination you can muster, your gifts will take you places that will amaze you."

LES BROWN

H ave you ever examined the ridge of a mountain range? It rises and falls at various intervals, growing to peaks and falling to valleys all along the way. No peak is exactly the same, nor does it rise to exactly the same elevation. It is a constant journey to reach the top—then another top—then another top of the mountain. Even when you reach the highest summit, there is always another mountain range to explore, and possibly even higher heights.

When I reflect on my life and the journey I've followed, I see very much the same. The journey doesn't always end in the absolute best of ways, and there's usually additional elevations to discover. The mountain range is always growing with new goals, new ideas, new perspectives, and new peaks to explore. It is a beautiful mission of discovering new paths to take and creating new and higher summits to reach.

There are a thousand stops along the way to enjoy the view, reach another goal, and learn new things. There are valleys we may face, but they only lead to better views and higher vistas, if we just continue moving. If we push to see what's ahead and not what's behind, we realize the mountain range is just one step after another to discover what's awaiting for us at the top.

My goals and dreams form my mountaintops of life. They vary in height and difficulty, but always push me to continue moving onward and upward. In our mountain climbing journey, some peaks may only be an hour hike; others may require years of training and some special equipment. Either way, they are all attainable! I *will* make it there if I just keep moving and climbing.

What does your mountain range look like? Really think about it. Do you have a range of peaks to reach? Or are most of your peaks flattened out from years of just letting them sit and erode? Have you reached what you consider your highest peak, or are you still at sea level, knowing you've got to start climbing?

Wherever you are, now is your time!

Listen to me now: *Wherever you are,* now *is* your time.

If you've fallen one too many times, we're going to start slow. If you have reached peak after peak, we're going to make even higher mountains. Wherever you are, the way is the exact same: one single step at a time.

Let's get started.

Building your Mountains
Small Goals

Let's start with the small goals. In terms of the hiking/mountain climbing visualization, these are the short hikes for an evening stroll. Not much elevation, you won't get tired; it's just a nice walk to stretch your legs. In life, these are the goals you may have deemed unimportant enough for your daily attention, or too small to be considered a "dream". They are tasks that might only take an afternoon or, at most, a couple days to complete. These are things that absolutely could help you long-term, but really mostly impact you in the moment. They are everyday accomplishments to celebrate: applying for a fun game show, learning how to cook a new dish, finding time in your day to spend reading a book instead of working. Where have you stopped short from doing that one extra project or pushing forward up that little hill? These smaller peaks can be scattered all throughout your mountain range—at the bottom, near the top, everywhere in between.

Mid-Range Peaks

Next are your mid-range peaks. For these trails you probably need to buy hiking boots. Nothing crazy, just something that requires a little more preparation than your casual evening stroll. There's a little more elevation now, but you might just get a little winded, nothing more. In life, these are the goals that might require a couple days to several weeks to really sink your teeth into, but are bigger life goals that will impact you both in that moment and after. These might be applying for a new job or quitting the one you're in. It might be clearing out your house of all the clutter you've held onto as a comfort. It might be starting the blog or podcast you've always wanted to have, but have been too scared to put yourself out there. These mid-range peaks fill in the gaps as we build our higher goals.

Tall Peaks

Growing even higher, we form your tall peaks. These peaks will take training to reach, and may require some rock-climbing equipment along the way, just in case the path gets too steep to walk. In life, they are goals that you know are within your ability to do, but it might require more stamina and preparation than you've been previously willing to give.

Typically, these are the goals people give up on most, because it takes longer to accomplish than we'd all prefer. They may take you a year or a few years to really reach the top. Have you always wanted to start a business but are too scared to leave your job security and don't know where to start? Have you wanted to record a song but didn't think you were good enough to be famous, so you gave up practicing? Have you always wanted to run a 10k but didn't think you could run that far? These higher goals require months and sometimes years of preparation and nurturing to reach. They are the goals you know you could do, but you might be too tired, scared, or not committed enough to keep climbing for the full duration. Include these higher peaks in your mountains.

The Summits

Finally, the summits—the highest peaks of the mountain range. These are the Mount Everests. You will need some oxygen tanks and will have to prepare for weeks, if not months, for varying conditions in the climb. These are the goals that are so high, they are hidden in the clouds. In fact, it might not even seem like you *could* reach them. In life, they are seemingly impossible and unachievable. These are the goals many people don't even include in their mountain range, because they may take five or more years to achieve. They might be something like going for a certificate or license, an advanced degree, or becoming a best-selling author or motivational speaker. Perhaps you dream of inventing the first mainstream land/air car. Maybe you will find the cure to cancer. Maybe you will start a company that grows into a $1B enterprise.

Make your summit dreams—those supposedly unreachable mountain tops—part of your outline as you look at your mountain ranges. In fact, I recommend you add as many summit dreams in as you can. These "lofty" dreams are the peaks that will keep you going, encourage you to keep pressing forward, and never stop believing in yourself. They are the peaks we will be pushing toward in this book, to get you excited about the possible in the seemingly impossible. You've already reached some goals, and now is the time to add even more.

If we only focus on what we can do here and now, we miss out on the wide open space that life has to offer to reach more, do more, get more, and scale more. Who's to say that in ten years, you won't have the money to fund that major project you've always dreamed of? How do you know you won't make that one connection that will launch you into an entirely different orbit of life? If that perceived summit isn't in your mountain range anymore, you might not even try.

I encourage you to take a few minutes or hours or days—however long it takes—to build out your mountain range. List it, sketch it, whatever you prefer. Make a range of goals with the best estimated timeline in mind, and don't let your own view of what's possible hold you back. We are on this journey together, and I encourage you to start by pushing yourself now.

Yes, you *are* able.

Building Your Mountains

Questions

1. Sketch your mountain range, including small, medium, and large peaks and summits (example below), and label each peak with a goal or dream. Include as many goals and dreams as you can think of!

2. What are some of the peaks and summits you have already achieved?

3. What are some of the highest summits you've ever dreamed of that seem unreachable to you?

4. Prioritize these summits and peaks. What are the top three you will focus on during this journey?

5. How would your life change if you accomplished some of these goals?

Building Your Mountains

Reflections

Chapter 2

Meeting Your Guide

"For there is always light, if only we're brave enough
to see it, if only we're brave enough to be it."

AMANDA GORMAN

At this point, you might be wondering: Who is this woman? How can I trust her to lead me up this mountain path?

Truth be told, I am an ordinary woman with an ordinary background, who learned over the years that the right mindset makes *all* the difference. I am here with you to share my experiences, and encourage you as you climb. I'm here to help you on your journey by teaching you everything I have learned along my own mountain range, in hopes that it might make your path smoother and more purposeful.

I wasn't handed advantages in life, I wasn't given a leg-up in any of my goals. With the circumstances I was given, I was able to face every day and make it my own. I wasn't handed extraordinary opportunities; it was the mindset I had that *made* those opportunities appear.

All of this is to say: *You can do it, too.*

So who am I?

I'm the great granddaughter of sharecroppers, who bought the farm they once worked. I am the granddaughter of farmers, who also owned a local construction company and convenience store, and built the church where many in their town of Kingstree, South Carolina, worshipped.

I'm the daughter of two of the wisest and most hard working people I've ever known. They have helped me make all the key decisions in my life. They are master logisticians, who managed the love, education, upbringing, and movement of thirteen people, without even having high school diplomas.

My mother kept the house running, and was a financial whiz. She invested and saved like no one I know. My father worked hard to provide. He was so proud of each of us, but was a frustrated man. He wanted to provide more for us, but faced many limitations.

I'm the sibling to ten: seven brothers and three sisters. We grew up in Murphy Homes (MH) Public Housing in Baltimore. We had five bedrooms for all thirteen people. I shared one bedroom with all three of my sisters, and only had my own room for about two months in between high school and college.

Our home did not have central air, and on the hottest nights of the summer, our neighborhood would lose electricity from around 9:00 p.m. to about 4:00 a.m. It was dark and hot and extremely difficult to have a good night's rest.

With so many people in the house, we had assigned bath times and weekly chores. I had kitchen duty every four weeks: clean the kitchen after dinner, which included washing and putting away dishes, wiping down counters, tables, chairs, appliances and cabinets, and mopping the floor. Every Saturday, I had to clean the bathroom (yuck). The toilet never moved, but with seven brothers, you would think the toilet rolled around the room!

My mom did laundry every day. We had a washing machine, but we did not have a dryer. All our clothes were hung out to dry, no matter if it was winter, spring, summer, or fall. All our meals were home-cooked, because it was not feasible to pay for thirteen people to eat out. We ate at one large kitchen table. We had big commercial-sized pots and serving spoons, and we never had leftovers.

Our neighborhood pool was an above-ground pool that fit about 10–12 people at one time—much too small for the number of people who wanted to use it. It wasn't a pool you went to for a swim; it was a pool you splashed in to cool off. No chairs or towels were provided. If you went with a group, one person had to stay out to watch your things, or they would be "borrowed".

We went to church every Sunday. I learned how to play the piano and organ from an elder there. I walked to her house for lessons, and practiced at home on a paper keyboard.

All of this is to say, I wasn't just handed opportunities. But I remember from when I was 7 years old, I learned in my Sunday school lessons that *nothing* was impossible with God. I walked out of that classroom each week knowing that I *could* do anything. While I learned the practical steps to apply as I grew, from that moment, I lived each day with the mindset that I was going to accomplish every dream I had, no matter what happened or what tried to stand in my way.

Because of that lesson, my whole life perspective changed. No matter the circumstances, my life was full of opportunity.

I am honored to have been a part of the community I grew up in, including all the neighbors that are now like part of my family. I am grateful to have grown up in such a loving family, from whom I learned so much: generosity, discipline, faith, understanding, determination, and so much more. I am blessed that even though we didn't have a lot, my parents and community offered me unconditional and ongoing support, opportunities to be exposed to the possibilities of my dreams, and unimaginable encouragement.

I wouldn't trade my upbringing for anything. I'm reminded of the once a year Orioles and what's now the Ravens games that I got to experience. I can never forget that each activity at "The Rec" (the neighborhood's central recreation facility) was treated as a big event, even if it was just getting together with friends to play ping-pong or watch a basketball game.

I became a member of the chess club. I learned about horseback riding. I was president of our 4-H club (the first inner-city 4-H club in the country). I got to choose where I went to school and chose Western High School, the first public all-girls school in the country. There, I made lifelong friends and was introduced to a rigorous academic program that truly stimulated my excitement to explore so many different things. I was actively engaged in church, which taught me who I am and whose I am.

I wanted to go away to college, and I'm so glad I did. I didn't go far, only a few hours to Frostburg State University. I chose the school because it was paid for. My parents had no money to send any of us to college, so this was an easy decision and ended up being one of the best decisions of my life. It was a fresh start from a new peak where I became more inquisitive. Classes were harder and challenging for me, but they helped me bloom. I shed being extremely shy and reserved and unsure of myself, and discovered I was able to walk away, run away or stand firm in my thoughts, aspirations, goals, and convictions. I also got to try activities I had never done before, like basketball, volleyball, and skiing.

After college, I worked at four dynamic and progressive companies before opening my first business. Since then, I have started four businesses. I have sold two businesses. In addition, I have also started multiple community initiatives and run non-profits for a variety of causes.

I am the wife of my staunchest supporter, who encourages me to always work towards reaching my goals and dreams, and is always by my side to witness their reveal.

> *It doesn't matter where you come from. You have something to give.*

I am the mother of two daughters, who attended Historically Black Colleges and Universities (HBCU) and are making a difference in the world. One daughter has launched her company and my other daughter has decided that she, too, is starting a business. I am also the grandmother of a future HBCU Class of 2033 graduate.

It doesn't matter where you come from. You have something to give.

Everything that was a part of me growing up, formed me into who I am today. Both the good and the not-as-good played a huge role in getting me where I am now. In fact, I named one of my companies after the street I grew up on: George Street. That community was instrumental in making me who I am, and though it may seem lacking, it was one of the richest places to learn, grow, and thrive. You probably wonder whatever happened to my beloved neighborhood? With the increase in drugs and their use, the ramifications destroyed MH. It became a drug-infested, unsafe neighborhood that was eventually imploded and replaced with new housing.

My father has since passed, and my mother is living with dementia, but still thriving. My siblings all have their own lives. Three have passed, three are retired, and the rest of us are either gainfully employed, underemployed, or unemployed. I am in regular contact with some of my siblings, and others not as often. I have ridden the waves of the highs and lows in life and have seen the tallest vistas and lowest valleys from my own mountain range.

But, no matter what comes my way, nothing distracts me from my goals. Nothing in my life has ever held me back or prevented me from achieving all of my craziest of dreams.

Many times, I feel like I'm doing the cha-cha: one step forward and two steps back. At times, I have felt confident, then less confident. Resilient, then less resilient. Formidable, then less formidable. Bold and also racked with fear. But throughout it all, one thing has always been constant: My faith which keeps me climbing, because in all I do, I make a difference to my family, my friends, my community, and the many nameless and faceless that I may never get to meet on this side of Heaven.

I went from child number six in my family to having the honor of being my mother's and some of my siblings' primary decision-maker. I went from being a ferocious reader about the world to traveling around the world. I went from being a software engineer to an entrepreneur. I am an ordinary person, who has climbed some high peaks to do some extraordinary things, and still has so much farther to reach.

I have found something interesting and inspirational in everyone I've met, every job I've held, and everything I've done. I believed then—and still believe now—that I am *able*, and so are *you*!

Thank you for taking an interest in me, my life, and my work. I hope I provide you with some inspiration and that you accept my invitation to join me as I join you in climbing your summit. I hope my words and life in some way speak to your heart, your mind, and your desire to reach your summit. You've only just begun, and I know you have so much more to accomplish.

Now . . . lace up! Let's begin climbing.

Meeting Your Guide

Questions

1. Who are *you*? How would you describe yourself? What are your strongest and greatest attributes?

2. What events have you gone through in life that made you who you are or brought you to the place you are now? Was there anything that happened that sent you on a different path than you expected in life?

3. When have you or did you step out of your comfort zone?

Meeting Your Guide

Reflections

Chapter 3

Forging Your Path

"Your life is your own. You mold it. You make it."

ELEANOR ROOSEVELT

We all think about what we want to be and what we want to do. It's a never-ending process. Growing up, most of us had big dreams with no limitations as to what was possible, what it would require, or how much money or time it would take. But still, we dreamed. As we age, most of us still have big dreams, but have put them on pause or have deemed them unreachable. What's changed?

Growing up, I wanted to be a major league baseball announcer, a programmer, a business owner and many other things, but one dream that always stuck with me was the dream of being an astronaut. The idea of going into space absolutely fascinated me! It was just so amazing watching all of the initial activity associated with the space program. The idea of people actually going into a part of the universe that we could only see glimpses of from the earth was something that danced through my mind day after day.

My college did not offer a computer science program at the time, which could have possibly been the perfect transition to my space career. Instead, I decided to follow another dream of mine—entrepreneurship—and majored in business administration. This decision made the most sense to help my career and bring me closer to my goals of owning businesses one day. Besides, not majoring in computer science wouldn't stop me from becoming an astronaut; I could easily go to grad school or have a double major that's relevant to the space industry (I later returned to school for a MBA with a focus in Technical Communications). More important to me was that college opened my mind to explore and define my options to become an astronaut and business owner.

My plan worked, and even without a computer science degree, my first job right out of college was as a software engineer. There was a large learning curve for me as a business major, but by working extra hours every day, I was quickly on par with my talented coworkers, who had started with more computer science knowledge. After a year, I changed companies and was hired by Space Communications Company which "launched" my career in the space industry. This was exactly the opportunity I had been hoping for.

I absolutely *loved* the company. I was given a lot of responsibility and authority, and worked closely with a NASA program every single day. Although I wasn't flipping in zero gravity, performing unique experiments, or eating dehydrated food, in many ways I felt like I was in training to be an astronaut. I was learning and was an integral part in the science of operating and communicating with actual satellites. I was witnessing the intricate details of space travel that not many have the opportunity to see. I was "in," and though I knew I was far from meeting the qualifications to be an astronaut, that high mountain peak felt closer and closer every single day.

After being with the company for just a short period of time, I was able to assist in one of the coolest projects I've had to date—supporting the launch of the first classified satellite, TDRS. As we watched that satellite reach its proper orbit, I felt like I was traveling along with it, up into the stars. All of the effort and passion of my small role left the earth with that launch. A piece of me *did* travel to space.

I may not have actually flown up into space (or, haven't yet), but I do feel that dream was fulfilled. I still picture myself very clearly in a space suit, flying in space. And, I'm not dissatisfied with what I was able to do, even if that's where it ends.

So often, we tend to place our dreams in certain molds. To accomplish them, it has to be a certain period of time or in a certain way or with a certain person. We see the one path up the mountain, but miss the rocks that we might be able to climb instead to reach a new level. We develop an image of what the view will look like from the top, but forget the view is constantly rotating 360° . . . just like those astronauts in zero gravity!

There is no right way to reach the top and accomplish your goals. There are endless paths up that mountain in your life! There is no perfect mold to any dream or goal you have. No, I didn't wear a space suit. But without our team that satellite would not have made it into the proper orbit in space in the first place.

The closer we get to our goals, the more we might see them shifting, realigning, and being reassessed. It is completely natural to have the same dream look completely different than you originally imagined, especially after several weeks or years. There's nothing wrong with that! You may find that the dream as you envisioned it years ago is not really what you want now, or it may just play out differently than you had originally thought.

The key is, *you* are the one who gets to make the mold. *You* are the one who decides what your dreams will look like. *You* are the shaper of your own destination.

In the same way you change the mold as you go, it is also up to you to make the mold to start. How many times have you felt you've grown stagnant because you're waiting for the right opportunity or the right situation to fall into your lap? Because you've envisioned how the plan should play out, you become frozen and unable to start when it doesn't look exactly like you imagined.

It becomes impossible to even make a step forward if you don't start making your own mold *now*.

Think about Sarah Blakely, the inventor of the greatest assist to women there is—*Spanx*. She made her own mold (literally and figuratively) from start to finish. When she saw a need in her own life, she cut the feet off pantihose and made her first "prototype" of what would become one of the most well-known brands of shaping undergarments out there. There was no blueprint for creating the products she imagined; she called factories for weeks trying to get them to work with her. She broke the mold over and over and over again to convince people that her products were worth it, and now she's made it to countless lists of the most successful women in the world.

I encourage you to start challenging yourself with this thought: *there is no mold.* No matter what you've told yourself in the past, you can be whatever and whoever you dream to be, by creating your own path along the way. From start to finish, stop putting your dreams in a box. Stop limiting yourself by creating a version of what the goal *should* look like, rather than what it *could* look like. See your dream beyond the picture frame holding you down. Make it happen, in whatever way you need. It *is* possible. It *is* doable, with the right mindset.

> *There is no perfect mold. Break down that box, and make your own way!*

In every dream, there is no perfect mold. Break down that box, and make your own way!

Forging Your Path

Questions

1. In my dream of being an astronaut for NASA, I found I had accomplished that goal in my own way through my job at Space Communications. Looking back on your life, where have you accomplished some of your big goals in a different way than you originally anticipated?

2. Your imagination is your best tool in forging your own path. When did you realize you have the power to dream, and what are those dreams?

3. When did you realize you have something special?

4. What are your hidden gifts or talents?

5. When you are unmotivated, what motivates you?

6. When you're at a point where it's going to be a tough climb, what do you bring along?

Forging Your Path

Reflections

Chapter 4

Overcoming Your Obstacles

"Life is about accepting the challenges along the way, choosing to keep moving forward, and savoring the journey."

ROY T. BENNETT

I wish I could tell you life happened the way I envisioned and I reached all the goals I set. I wish I could tell you life fell in line and all I had to do was follow my GPS instructions. I wish I could say there are no detours and struggles when you adjust your mindset and forge ahead, but to be honest, that's just not true.

Truth is, when you're climbing a mountain, you'll more than likely hit some rough trails. It's a mountain, after all! The snags all look different—it might be some thorny branches that catch your shirt, a rock that trips you up, or a pond of water or rock wall that blocks your path ahead.

We've talked a lot about the achievements—the successes, the peaks, the high points in life. But what about the times where things go wrong? What about the times you feel defeated, like everything is working against you?

As much as I talk about the successes in my life, I've also faced challenges. No matter how positive my attitude was, not everything went as planned. I could prepare as much as possible, but at the end of the day, life happens.

A few years ago, I got a call that halted my life with just three words: "You have cancer." This wasn't just some thorny branches; this was a massive pile of trees in my way; a rock face that had erected itself in an instant. It was a moment that stopped all my plans and made me change my focus. Instead of running my business for the following two years, I was fighting for my life. Instead of visiting with my family and friends in their big moments, I was laying in bed recovering from chemo. Instead of creating new organizations and starting new projects, I was dealing with the changes in my physical appearance and trying not to let the doctors' saddened looks affect my positive outlook.

It was clear to me that I had a slim chance of survival. Thanks to the incredible experience and collaboration and innovation of the medical team, I made it. But it certainly wasn't easy. To have such an aggressive form of cancer (or any form of cancer, for that matter) is not something you recover from overnight. It's not an obstacle that disappears once you're "clear". I am still going through surgeries and healing, even to this day, and I may still be going through it years from now.

It was a solid rock wall—*still* is a wall—on my mountain to scale. There was no getting around it or through it; I had to climb over with all the strength I had, letting people lift me up along the way when I couldn't bring myself to handle it. The path I was climbing in my career and my life at that point disappeared. Even now, it's a path that has been ever-changing and evolving. Some parts of the path, I've had to step around and leave behind. Others, I've had to rebuild or remake. My life and my mountain range may never look the exact same as it had before.

I've had several other snags and obstacles throughout my life: being looked down on because of my childhood neighborhood, facing trials as an entrepreneur, and being an African-American woman in a primarily male-dominated industry.

All of these snags along my mountain trail are not things I could control. They're parts of my life and who I am. They're elements of my story that either popped up as challenges or became challenges because of the perspective of others.

When I grew up in my neighborhood, I never thought it was a negative. I loved my community. Having others look down on it or think poorly of it was not easy to swallow. Having friends say they couldn't come visit me because of where I lived was hard to understand as a child. Seeing the reaction people had when I talked about my neighborhood, even as I grew up, was frustrating. My neighborhood helped shape me into who I am today. It may not have been the wealthiest community, but that didn't detract from the beauty it held, and remembering that throughout my developing years was key to holding on to the lessons I learned, the people I loved, and the memories I cherished.

In my business life, I had a partner betray me, competitive companies attempt to raid my business and take all my employees.

The success of my business and career wasn't an easy walk in the park. These challenges fell like large trees in my path—suddenly and frighteningly trying to stop me.

In my everyday life, the judgement and challenges that come from being an African-American woman are constant snags that catch my clothes. Most of them are twigs that snap off or small thorns I can easily cast aside, but they do regularly remind me that they are there, no matter what I do.

My life hasn't been an easy climb, and I don't say that to discourage you; I say that to *encourage* you. I never want to disregard the challenges I've faced, because they are a part of my story. In fact, I would argue that the times I've had to scale walls or find another path have actu-

> *No matter what walls stop you in your tracks, your mindset matters!*

ally pushed me further than I would have originally gone. Being forced to face the challenges has made me stronger and has given me a drive to create *more* mountains and get started on the paths I might have otherwise forgotten or left for later.

I have learned (and hope you can too) that no matter what life throws at you—no matter what branches fall in your path unexpectedly or what walls try to stop you in your tracks—*your mindset matters*! Ultimately, all you can control when things come your way is how you respond to them.

I have always told my friends, "When you put up a fence [or a rock wall, in our mountain analogy], I'm going to figure out how to get over, under or around it." Approaching each new challenge with that mindset means that I *will* get over it. The solution won't look the same every time, but I *will* make it to the other side.

There will *always* be challenges. I've had so many challenges,

I can't even remember them all! Life is not a one-dimensional event that only travels in one direction. Like your mountain range or a wave in the ocean, it ebbs and flows, falling and rising in each new moment. I hope and pray that every challenge you face is just a little twig—an annoyance at best—that's easy to ignore and move on. But I can't guarantee that for either of us! Life is a journey.

So how do we change our mindset when challenges come that are out of our control?

1) Tell yourself that you *will* make it. No matter how bleak it looks, you *will* get to the other side. Your attitude determines your success!

2) Assess the challenge. Figure out for yourself: Is this an annoying twig or branch, or a new wall in my path? Is it something that will disappear in a moment, or something that has changed how I must approach my climb? To go back to the old saying, recognize the difference between a mountain and a molehill. How large is the challenge, what does it affect, and what is the best way to approach getting to the other side?

3) Put a plan in place. If you find that your challenge is just a twig, continue forward and know it is only there for a moment. If you come to realize that your challenge is a large obstacle or rock wall, form a plan: Do you want to go over, around, or under the wall?

Sometimes, climbing the wall is exactly what you need to do—keep pushing forward, get over the wall, and make it to the other side. Build your strength and keep pushing. It may be the very thing you need to build some endurance for your next big climb.

Sometimes, getting around the wall is the best option—see where the wall is, where it ends, and what angles you can approach from. Sometimes, this does mean leaving the challenge altogether. That doesn't mean you quit; it means there are some points in your life that are meant to reroute you and make you reassess. Sometimes you *do* hit a deadend through the challenges, and that's okay! If by reassessing you find there is another path waiting for you, go around the wall and start your new path.

Sometimes, the wall requires innovative thinking to get *under* it to the other side. It requires thinking outside the box to find the solution, and letting yourself get a little

> *There are some points in your life that are meant to reroute you.*

uncomfortable in order to dig your way through. It may not be a solution most people attempt, but it may be exactly what you need. Find an alternate solution and push yourself in new ways and use new skills to get it done and continue on your journey.

4) Be present. Sometimes it gets strenuous, sometimes you get exhausted. If you put forth all the necessary energy and make it to the other side, you will get recharged and your view will be wider. It could even show you a better way to approach some of your taller summits! Take it all in—the challenging situation— and use the clarity of the path you've just cleared to help you get to the next stage. Doing steps 1, 2, and 3 helps you get to the point of being present and truly ready to climb the tall peaks, summits, etc. Your endurance grows, your confidence increases, and your ability to say, "It's okay, I have this, and I'm going to make it," becomes more and more natural.

There's *always* a way. No matter what comes your way, know that you *will* make it to the other side. You *will* come out better and stronger for it, and may find yourself on a new path that's even better than the one before it! No matter what happens, don't let challenges bring you down. It's a new adventure, a new journey, a new moment to prove yourself and show how far you've come. Don't let those moments slip by; embrace them and discover all that you can do.

Overcoming Your Obstacles

Questions

1. List out some of the challenges you've faced in terms of mountain obstacles: thorny branches (annoying snags), ponds of water (challenges that change your path), or rock walls (challenges that temporarily halt your journey).

    a. Which of these obstacles have you already overcome? How did you overcome these?

    b. What are some obstacles still standing in your way? How do you plan to overcome these?

2. Is there a common theme to many of the challenges you've faced? Is there anything you can do now to prevent them from reoccurring in the future?

Overcoming Your Obstacles

Reflections

_____

_____

_____

_____

_____

_____

_____

_____

_____

_____

_____

_____

_____

_____

_____

_____

_____

Chapter 5

Removing Your Constraints

"Life has no limitations, except the ones you make."

LES BROWN

In October of 2001, I thought my business was going under. Although we were financially sound, a rumor began that we were having challenges and ran the risk of going out of business. The real issue became what I perceived as the other employees' lack of vision, investment, and belief in the company and myself as their leader. With our financial status in question, many rumors started about the stability of the company. Many employees began leaving for what they thought would be more job security. I assured them many times that we could do it, that it was just a season, that we would get through it. Still, employees continued to leave.

What I witnessed in those months was an enlightening truth: When you are rumored to be having financial challenges (even in the midst of never missing a payroll), no matter what you say, people will believe what they want to believe, and you will inevitably begin doubting yourself as well. Really, on a broader scale, no matter what you say about any issue in general, people will believe what they want to believe. And that got me thinking: Where did the thoughts or the truths I believed in my life actually come from?

I often think about when I opened my business in 1996 and I thought I was reaching for the stars by wishing for my first million dollar contract. Nobody *told* me that was an impossible goal. People may have had their opinions that influenced me, but really—who placed that dream in the sky instead of right in front of me in a fully attainable spot? I did. When I believed that I couldn't have multiple companies, who told me that? I did. When I thought there was no way I could produce a song, who told me that? I did. When I admired runners and thought there was no way I could run a 5k, who put that wall up? I did.

Looking through all the doubts in my life, I realized an interesting truth: *I* was the one who developed them. People will offer up their advice, thoughts, and opinions all the time. Ultimately, at the end of the day, I'm going to believe what I want to believe and use what I want to use. I choose how to receive it and what to do with it. The limits you allow in your life are the only ones that truly make an impact.

Taking it back to October of 2001, I had been focusing on everything that was going wrong. There was so much information coming at me. It would have been so easy to just give up and say, "You know what? This is too much. I'm tired." But I had decided long ago that I won't give up. I knew I could make things work. I could handle it, and I put a plan in place and got to work. I decided to receive all information, then quickly make a decision on how to use it. I either passed it on to someone else for their use, moved forward with the information for my use, classified it as useless information and threw it away, or continued to analyze the information for further consideration.

If I had given in to the negative thoughts and information that were swirling around me, then we would not have been named the 7th fastest growing business in Washington Technology Fast 50 (*Washington Technology*, 2002) exactly one year later. If I didn't believe my company could win million dollar contracts, I would not have been awarded my first contract (and many more million dollar contracts to follow). If I didn't believe that I could own multiple successful companies, I would have missed out on not only owning multiple businesses, but also the opportunities they afforded me of helping others grow their careers, helping others launch their companies, and coordinating community service initiatives like "Just a Kind Note."

We all have our own set of limiting beliefs that we have placed on ourselves. Backing away from fulfilling a dream or blaming others for the limiting thoughts is the *easy* way out. It's so convenient to place the fault on the things we can't control or the people in our lives who have impacted us negatively. In reality, there's no limit to what we can do.

Since we're on this mountain together, let's think about these self-limiting beliefs as your perspective of the mountain's size. We may see the mountain and think it's at a distance, much larger than we could ever scale. Or, we may look at the rocks and difficult trek and think the climb requires skill that far surpasses our own.

Sometimes, we disguise our self-limiting beliefs as "caution" to make ourselves feel better. We rationalize that holding back is for our safety and security, when really it's just fear keeping us from where we're meant to go.

Think about when you were a child—how large did everything seem to you at that time? Dogs that may be cute adorable puppies as an adult seemed like massive beasts as a child. The idea of having a job seemed like such a far-off reality when we were 5 years old, but is a part of everyday life as an adult.

> *Sometimes we disguise our self-limiting beliefs as "caution" to make ourselves feel better.*

Perspective is everything.

Imagine seeing a mountain off in the distance. How accurate can you assess the size of the mountain, when you have no reference? You may dismiss the mountain as massive when, in reality, seeing it up close proves it's just a small hill. Similarly, when you begin training for something—a job, a physical task, a long journey—the end result may be daunting. However, as you train and grow, the final goal seems more and more feasible.

It's time to throw our caution to the wind and remove the constraints we have placed on our lives. With the right perspective and attitude, we cannot be stopped.

I decided very early on in my life that "no" was not an option for me, because it gave me an "out." It was an easy way to say "I can't do it," or "I won't do it." The truth was, I *could* and I *would*. I *would* run multiple companies. I *would* start multiple charitable organizations. I *would* organize to raise millions of dollars for cancer research and patient care. I *would* become a ballroom dancer. I *would* survive. I *would* thrive. I *would* make it to the top of my mountain. I *would*, I *would*, I *would*.

No matter how difficult or challenging, I would make it through. When I was diagnosed with cancer, I *knew* I was going to survive. When my business faced challenges, I *knew* I would make it. When I decided to venture into writing and speaking, I *knew* I would see it through.

And I did.

I have signed multiple million dollar contracts and am now aiming for a $50 million contract. I run multiple companies. I survived cancer. I brought my company through some of the hardest financial troubles I could have anticipated. I have completed projects that are positioning me for a new chapter of my career.

I did it, and not because of some great stroke of luck. I did it because I *said* I would and I *knew* I would.

I stopped thinking everything has to be perfect. Instead, I get joy out of watching what I started evolve into better products and services.

I stopped trying to please everyone and get everyone's opinion and input. Instead, I use the information I have and make the best decision with my trusted team.

I stopped including dream slayers in my decision process. You know, the people who tell you why you can't or won't or shouldn't do something. Instead, I surround myself with people who believe in me and believe I can do it, and will help guide me along the way. I stopped letting distractions creep into my vision and cleared the path to keep my goals in sight.

It's time to toss our self-limiting beliefs and start giving ourselves the pep talk we need. Let's break down those self-built barriers and begin living our lives like we won't fail. Sometimes, things might not go as planned, but that doesn't mean we stop. We keep going, we keep pushing, we keep pressing on and never let ourselves think for even a minute that we can't.

We *can*. And we *will*.

Removing Your Constraints

Questions

1. Name three self-limiting beliefs or negative thoughts you've developed through the years.

   a. How did they get there? How can or did you get rid of them?

2. List some of the descriptions and traits you've believed about yourself that aren't true.

3. What are some distractions that have crept into your vision and need to be cleared to see your goals ahead? How can you clear those out now, before they become a problem?

4. Now that you've removed your negative thoughts and self-limiting beliefs, what dreams are you excited to pursue?

Reflections

_____

_____

_____

_____

_____

_____

_____

_____

_____

_____

_____

_____

_____

_____

_____

_____

Chapter 6

Creating Your Squad

"We should always have three good people in our lives-one who walks ahead, who we look up to and follow; one who walks beside us, who is with us every step of our journey; and then, one who we reach back for and bring along after we've cleared the way."

MICHELLE OBAMA

*D*ing! *Ding ding ding ding!*
Mama's dinner bell was the signal of excited chaos in our house. As soon as the bell rang, the rush to the food began. We all knew that with thirteen people (plus any friends who stayed for dinner), you had to get there fast to get your fair share of Mama's

delicious homemade cooking.

It seems like it was yesterday. I can still picture it so vividly: Me, curled up in a chair in my bedroom reading my latest novel, the bell ringing in the distance, the smell of Mama's cooking already coming up to where I sat. I always had my nose in a book, so the dinner bell was brought in just for me. If I didn't hear the call, my brothers would eat up all the food. We never had leftovers!

I'd quickly mark the spot where I stopped in my book and race down to the kitchen to await my plate. We all had assigned seats at the table, but that didn't stop any of our friends from trying to steal a seat. My brother's friend, Matthew, in particular, was very persistent. Only when one of the siblings was missing did that ever work.

The thirteen seats around the table were filled with my parents and siblings, and any friends who stayed sat in any of the other empty chairs in the room. After blessing the food—the one quiet moment of all our meals—then every conversation you could imagine began, many times all at once.

On one end of the table, my brothers and father might be discussing the latest sports game. On the other side, my mother might be talking to my sister about her latest boyfriend or her participating in an upcoming church program. Me, I might be telling my siblings about the book I'm reading, my latest ideas, or negotiating chores with one of my brothers.

It was a whole mix of conversations in the most beautiful way. I learned so much at that table: how to express my ideas and opinions, how to talk with a large group, how to negotiate, how to encourage others, and so much more. It was an open table with the opportunity to speak your mind and find out who you are. It was fun.

My siblings and I, even though we have the same parents and

grew up in the same house under the same guidance, are all completely different. I cannot think of two of us who are alike. While that could be chaos at times, it brought out the best discussions when talking through what could be a touchy subject. It brought new ideas to the table that some of us had never thought of, and introduced a range of thinking that I would never have on my own. It also brought lots of laughter all the time.

The table was a magical place, looking back on it. Those family meals helped shape me as a person, in both my personal and professional lives. It was a backbone to so many situations in my life that I had to navigate.

It set me up for success. And now, I get to set my own table.

Yes, I set my table for my family meals. But in a broader sense, I set my "table" for my life, and I invite people to come share a meal with me. Just like my family dinner meals, the meetings are regular (we're always in communication), and offer a safe place to share my thoughts and dreams. No, we may not be literally sharing meals together, but I consider each one of them a crucial part of shaping me and changing the trajectory of my life.

In the climb to my mountaintops, these people create the squad who have helped me reach the peaks. Some are part of my training inside, some go on shorter walks with me, others climb all the way to the top with me, holding my rope when I need to scale some walls. They all play a different role, but each role is so uniquely important.

Through every season, they are my support system, confidants, encouragers and reality checks. They are people I trust with my entire being, knowing that they are standing by my side no matter what. They have seen my struggles but mostly, know what I am capable of and continuously encourage me to get there.

I sit at my "table" and "climb" with my squad to share my dreams, air out my thoughts, and talk through my perspectives on everything that I'm going through. No matter what, I know that the people there are in front of me, beside me, and behind me through thick and thin.

So who's on your squad? Who do you have in your life right now who are there when you need them, to offer a perspective, help you train, or keep pushing you forward?

The spots on your squad are reserved. Just like my family dinner table, there are assigned seats. While there may be many people in the room, who are your special few that have a seat at your table, no matter what?

Your answer won't always stay the same. People may come and go from your squad as life moves you forward, and that's okay. Sometimes, people change. Sometimes, *you* change. There are seasons for everything and everyone. Who you may need in your life right now won't be the same people you need five years from now, when you are in an entirely different time of life.

> *People may come and go from your squad as life moves you forward, and that's okay.*

I don't think my squad has had the same people in it for more than two years at a time. People move, grow, and change into different roles in your life; it's not a bad thing to change the seating arrangement. I've had several people I thought would be on my team forever, who are now either sitting in an empty chair along the wall or haven't been invited in the room in a while. We're all people, and we're always changing. It's important to know who you need now and what's most important to you in each season of life.

One of the elements I value most from having a squad of people is that, just like my siblings, none of us think or feel or even look exactly the same. Every person with a seat has a different mindset, a different perspective, a different value that they bring. It's a value far above any other, to surround yourself with people you respect and who bring a lot for you in your life.

Now, I'm not suggesting you go out and find people who will always think the opposite of you. It's important to know who and what you need. For example, I have a rule that to have a spot on my squad, you must be a positive person. For me, negativity (very different than disagreeing or having a different perspective) does not help me grow. However, outside of that, the people in my life and on my squad come from different backgrounds, have different beliefs, and love different things than I do. They help keep me well-rounded.

Your squad is a key to your success. Start thinking through who is helping you climb your mountains. Are they truly helping you climb or are they holding you back from the greater things in store? It's time to take a look at your squad, and figure out who's coming and who has to stay behind.

Creating Your Squad

Questions

1. Who is your squad? List at least 3 people who hold you accountable to pursuing your goals.

   a. Why are they a part of your squad? How are they similar? How are they different?

2. Who else do you think could be an important part of your squad? What expertise, personality traits, or strengths might benefit your squad?

3. Is there anyone in your squad you should remove?

Creating Your Squad

Reflections

_____
_____
_____
_____
_____
_____
_____
_____
_____
_____
_____
_____
_____
_____
_____
_____
_____
_____

Chapter 7

Finishing Your Climb

"Many of life's failures are people who did not realize how close they were to success when they gave up."

THOMAS EDISON

A friend once told me about one of her favorite shows—*The Amazing Race*. If you're not familiar with it, it's a show where eleven teams of two race around the world completing tasks and finding clues to direct them along the way. The first place team at the end of the season wins $1 million!

In one particular episode she was telling me about, there was a task where the teams had to find hidden treasure. They were given a compass, a set of directions, and a shovel that measured exactly one yard. Their directions might have read: Start at the anchor. N 15, W 24. In that case, the team would measure 15 yards north from the anchor, and then 24 yards west from that point. Once they completed the directions, they should have been on the spot where their treasure was located.

Since I was curious, I decided to watch the episode myself. It seemed easy enough at first. No directions were incredibly long or challenging; the most difficult part seemed to be figuring out how to read a compass. Let me tell you, these teams *struggled*. Some of them searched for *hours* out on that beach, trying to find their treasure chest!

Discouraged and tired, each of the last three teams debated taking a four-hour penalty (standard rule in the race) to avoid having to finish their task. As they each talked with their partners, the show gave us a glimpse of where their treasure actually was in relation to them. They were steps—*steps*—away from their treasure chest. Each and every one of them were only 1–2 yards away!

They had come so close to their treasure chests, but gave up. Because they gave up on the task, all three teams had to race to the finish line, and the team who came in last was eliminated from the race. The other two teams, though they were still in the race, were at a four-hour disadvantage from all of the other teams, who had completed the challenge.

Looking back on it, I'd bet the teams who took the penalty regretted their decision. Seeing how far they had come and how close they were to the treasure (the team who was eliminated was only about 1 foot away) probably made them wish they had tried just one more time, or searched just a little bit more. We sure did, watching it! I wanted to shout at the television, telling the teams to try again! They were so close! It would have saved them time, stress, and, for one team, the chance at the $1 million prize.

Isn't this how we operate in life, though? How many times have you quit something because it's too hard, too stressful, too tiring? You might not have seen any result happening right away, so it seemed like the result you wanted would never occur. It'd be better to quit while you're ahead and not waste any more time, right? *Wrong.*

Just like the teams on *The Amazing Race*, maybe your treasure—your goal, your dream, the final piece in your accomplishment—was waiting just *one step* away from you. Maybe, with one more attempt or one more day or one more push to finish, you would have reached the peak of your mountain.

Instead, you stopped just short of the peak. Maybe you were climbing through some foliage and couldn't see that the top was just ahead where the treeline broke. Maybe you reached a small side peak and decided that was far enough; the view seemed okay. But if you had just kept climbing, the view at the top would have been spectacular.

So many times, we stop short of our goals *just* before we would have reached them. Of course, we don't always know that at the moment. Unfortunately, we don't have a television crew following us around, who knows our lives to the detail, including things that haven't happened yet. No one can tell us exactly how long our goals will take or how we need to get there.

One. More. Step.

Throughout my life, I have grown up with, worked with, and watched so many people who are more creative, intelligent, and talented than myself give up on their dreams and miss out on degrees, job opportunities, and wild dreams. I can see from the outside perspective that they are so close, but when they can't see the treasure buried in the sand beneath their feet, it seems impossible. They possess everything they need to win! If they had just kept pushing for one more day, one more step, they would have made it, and their lives may have been completely different.

Now, all of this is not to say that a dream or goal can't change over time. Many might argue that the teams on *The Amazing Race* made a very strategic decision to give up on finding that treasure chest that they couldn't manage to find, so they could make it to the finish line in some way or another.

It's true that, as we discussed, dreams and goals are always shifting, changing, and being reassessed. You might have a goal one minute that ends up looking completely different in the next moment. The paths are always changing. Always take the time to sit and examine your goals, where you are, and where you're headed. If in your reassessment you discover that there is a new path that better fits your time in life, take it! If in your reassessment you discover it's the wrong path, it's okay to leave it behind. However, if you know that this is the right path and it's just harder to do than you anticipated, keep going!

Changing and shifting your goals is different than giving up. You can reassess your goals every single day and continue creating your own molds. You can shift your perspective and find a different path. But don't give up on where you're meant to be just because it's hard!

Your breakthrough might be *one step away*. Now is *not* the time to quit. That mountaintop might be just over the ridge! You may not see it, but it is there. Your time is *coming*. You have nothing to lose!

Keep going!

I know you might feel tired and exhausted, like going one more step would push you over the edge. But just think about the alternative! If you go your whole life without trying one more step, one more push, one more attempt, you may always wonder the dreaded, "*What if?*" You may find yourself, years from now, farther away from your goal than ever before, because you got too tired when you were so close.

As many of you may already know, life never slows down. There is never a moment where everything pauses to give you a respite and let you do all the things you ever wanted to do. Your time is *now*! Grab that chance while you have it. Take that opportunity while it is right in front of you. When the doubts rush in that your destination doesn't exist or you are running out of time, don't let it get to you! No matter what, you have all the time in the world. You are the maker of your own destiny. You can choose to try one more time and take one more step, or you can take that penalty and the possibility of losing out on what you were made to do.

> *You are the maker of your own destiny.*

Now is your time. You've got this! I am here with you, supporting you all the way. One step at a time, *don't give up*! We will walk it together and get you to that breakthrough point. Let's take it *one more step*, and I promise you—you *will* reach your goal and see the magnificent view at the top.

Finishing Your Climb

Questions

1. What are some of your dreams and goals that you have . . .

   Put on hold?
   Given up on?
   Redirected?

2. Which dreams do you need to just take one more step and keep pushing forward to try to finish it up?

   What steps can you take today?

Finishing Your Climb

Reflections

Chapter 8

Celebrating Your Journey

"The great victory, which appears so simple today, was the result of a series of small victories that went unnoticed."

PAULO COELHO

In the Spring of 2010, my daughter told me she was pregnant with my first grandchild. I was *so* excited that I was going to be a grandmother, I decided to hold a Grandmother's Brunch. There were invitations sent out, delicious food ordered, and decorations made. I went above and beyond for this brunch.

I invited all my friends and wrote on the invitation, "You are invited to my naming rights—should I be called 'Queen', 'Dutchess', 'Princess', 'Grandma' or some other royal name?" and ended with, "I'm going to be a grandmother. Kolbi's having a baby!" That was how all of my friends found out that Kolbi (my daughter) was pregnant. No, *I* wasn't pregnant; *she* was pregnant. And she wasn't even invited to this brunch! This was *my* celebration for becoming a grandmother. Of course, we had celebrations for Kolbi and my soon-to-be granddaughter as well, but the Grandmother's Brunch was just for me.

I celebrate *everything*. Down to the littlest detail, I celebrate. I don't think we, as a society, celebrate enough. We celebrate the standard things (like birthdays, graduations, baby showers, etc.), but we don't think outside the box to celebrate (like me becoming a grandmother).

When you look at your daily life, there are a thousand things to celebrate. It doesn't have to be a lavish event like my brunch or birthday party (I hosted over 350 friends for my 50th!). It can be something small, like a happy dance or a scream of delight or a nice lunch you buy yourself. You might be celebrating an extra 30 minutes of work you put into a project, the latest craft you created, or a phone call from an old friend. Whatever it is and whatever it looks like, celebrate! When you acknowledge the present moment, it leads to so many reasons to celebrate. Life is challenging, so why not reward yourself?

Ever since I was a little girl, one of my biggest dreams ever was to play basketball. Growing up with seven brothers, I watched, studied, and learned every sport there was (baseball, basketball, football, lacrosse, hockey, golf, wrestling . . . you name it). Sports were *always* on TV at my house.

I was the only family member who never played any sport

when I was young (the idea of all the bumping and sweating just wasn't appealing to me), but when I got to college, the opportunity presented itself: intramural sports. You didn't have to have any experience, you didn't have to know what you were doing; you just had to show up to practice and play. I never missed a practice.

I showed up to the first game in style: matching outfit, with long sleeves, my hair slicked back, the number "7" blazing proud, and a full set of elbow and knee pads to complete the ensemble. For the first two games, my coach never put me in. Finally, in the fourth quarter of my third game, my coach called me to go on the court. In the shining moment of my basketball career, I caught one pass and shot one layup.

As I watched the ball *swoosh* through the basket, you would have thought I won the Super Bowl. I jumped up and down, screaming that I had scored, celebrating every single part of the moments I had spent practicing those layups that led to this pinnacle moment. Only when the coach yelled, "Theresa! Get down the court!" (and had to call a time-out on my behalf) did I realize that my entire team was on the other end of the court, continuing the game.

That one layup in college was a big success in my basketball career (which ended just after that game) that I still celebrate all these years later. Even though I never was a WNBA star or on a college team, I still played basketball and even scored points in a game! The victories don't always look like you imagine they will, but celebrating the small stuff reaffirms you're doing what you want and you're on the right track.

In our mountain range, we can get so focused on the main peaks and summits that we forget to celebrate the small goals and accomplishments along the way.

Even though it was just one game and a layup, I reached the peak of my basketball dream that day. It was a small victory that was ultimately the fulfillment of my dream. But there are so many other dreams that are higher and harder to reach. This is where celebrating the small victories comes in handy the most. There are small victories along the path to our dreams that normally go completely unacknowledged, but should be celebrated. When you're trying to establish something or get something set up, the small celebrations help keep you wanting to climb to the next level.

Some of the tasks you do, some of the goals you achieve, some of the mountains you climb don't change the world. They may not even change your life, but celebrating them can put a smile on your face and build up your confidence to keep moving forward. Just being able to put a positive spin on your day can make a huge difference in your attitude and motivation and continuing your climb.

Picture a high mountain peak or summit—the big dreams you have in your life. The longer you climb, the further you are from the ground and the closer you are to the summit. Each small step you take will help you get to the top. If our dreams are the top of the mountains, the small goals are stepping stones and rock ledges as markers along the way.

Celebrate those little moments! Be aware, be excited, and keep on moving!

Be Aware

Each moment of every day, be aware of what is happening. Recognize when a moment is a reason to celebrate. Did you land a meeting with a client or decision-maker you've been trying to reach, who will help your business? Did you finally buy that treadmill you've wanted to get to begin your health journey? Did you pick up that guitar for the first time in years and strum a few chords? Every small moment can be a victory, if you are aware that they are happening.

If you struggle with finding the small victories, begin by celebrating other people's victories. Look at your friends and family, who surround you daily. Or even people you don't know! See what

If you struggle with finding small victories, begin by celebrating other people's victories.

victories they may have in their lives, and begin brainstorming how to celebrate them.

I can't tell you how many friends I've hosted dinners for, who have gotten a promotion, received a healthy doctor's report after an accident, met their future spouse, or any other reason under the sun. By recognizing it in others, you get to celebrate with them and practice recognizing those moments in *yourself.*

Be Excited

As you recognize these moments, it's time to celebrate! It might look different for you than it does for me, but the celebrations are what matter the most. A happy dance or song, an excited phone call to a friend, or a fancy dinner to spoil yourself—whatever it looks like, it is a celebration!

Bring others from your squad in to celebrate with you, as well! Sometimes, having others celebrating with you and supporting you keeps you accountable to keep moving forward. When I started running, I got so excited to even run a couple blocks that

I shared it with all my closest friends and family. Eventually, with the support and encouragement of my squad and community, I ran a 5k!

Once you recognize the moments that matter (no matter how small), don't be afraid to share them and celebrate.

Keep On Moving

Each celebration is a motivator to reach the next one. Every time you see yourself checking off a goal or accomplishing another step, use that excitement to propel you forward!

For the first time in this journey together, I want you to look *backwards* down the mountain. I want you to see the distance you've traveled. I want you to realize how far you've come. Look at the rough patches along the way and realize that you made it through! See the moments where you were climbing straight up a rock face. You made it to the ledge! Examine the portions of the path you can hardly see anymore, because they were and are so overgrown with foliage. You made it through! No matter how far you think the top might be, you have come *so* far! That in itself is a reason to celebrate.

Don't be afraid to look back, because it only shows you that you *can* do it. You have made it this far, and you can keep going and moving forward into the dreams that you have planned.

This is your call forward. *This* is your time. *This* is the moment you have trained for, looked for, and dreamed of for so long. Celebrate what you have accomplished today, and then keep moving forward.

You, my friend, are off to live your dreams.

Celebrating Your Journey

Questions

1. What was the last victory you celebrated? How did you celebrate?

2. What will you celebrate this week?

3. What upcoming goal or dream celebration are you looking forward to?

4. Who can you invite along to celebrate your victories with you?

Celebrating Your Journey

Reflections

I'm off and running,
and I'm not turning back.

PHILIPPIANS 3:14 (MSG)

Not that I have already obtained all this,
or have already arrived at my goal, but I press on
to take hold of that for which Christ Jesus took
hold of me. Brothers and sisters, I do not consider
myself yet to have taken hold of it. But one thing
I do: Forgetting what is behind and straining
toward what is ahead, I press on toward the goal
to win the prize for which God has called me
heavenward in Christ Jesus.

PHILIPPIANS 3:12–14 (NIV)

About the Author

Theresa Harrison is the co-author of a *Wall Street Journal, USA Today*, Amazon bestselling book, *BUSINESS SUCCESS SECRETS: ENTREPRENEURIAL THINKING THAT WORKS*. As a stimulating, action-driven speaker, she is sought after by organizations looking to motivate and encourage others.

Over a successful 25+ year career, Theresa has held executive and technical management positions. She is founder and president of GEORGE STREET Services, Inc.; former co-founder, president of Athenyx, LLC; and the founder of "Just A Kind Note," Hood College Board of Trustees, Truist Western Maryland Advisory Board, Woman to Woman Mentoring, Delta Sigma Theta Sorority, Inc, GEORGE STREET Foundation, and a variety of community service initiatives. Theresa mentor's future entrepreneurs and business leaders to increase the number of women and underrepresented business owners and technology experts.

For more information visit:
thgives.com | georgestreetinc.com | justakindnote.com
linkedin.com/in/theresa-harrison-148a3628

Rebecca Mitchell
rebeccamitchellwrites.com
connect@rebeccamitchellwrites.com

Don't Miss the Rest of the *Yes, You Are* Series!

Yes, You Are Resilient
Facing and embracing life's challenges as opportunities for a positive pivot

Yes, You Are Different
The power, freedom, and benefits of being you

Yes, We Are Boomers
A comical look into the lives and minds of the Boomer generation

Yes, You Are Starting Out
Methods and tips on starting on your desired path when endless opportunities lay before you

Yes, You Are Greeting Cards

Publishing in 2022 and 2023

Made in the USA
Columbia, SC
13 November 2022

71135244R00069